Pomegranate Odyssey

Hannah Calkin

Pomegranate Odyssey

Hannah Calkin

POMEGRANATE ODYSSEY
Copyright©2019 Hannah Calkin
All Rights Reserved
Published by Unsolicited Press
Printed in the United States of America.
First Edition.

All rights reserved. Printed in the United States of America. No part of this book may be used or reproduced in any manner whatsoever without written permission except in the case of brief quotations embodied in critical articles or reviews.

Attention schools and businesses: for discounted copies on large orders, please contact the publisher directly.

For information contact:
Unsolicited Press
Portland, Oregon
www.unsolicitedpress.com
orders@unsolicitedpress.com
619-354-8005

Cover Design: Kathryn Gerhardt
Editor: S.R. Stewart

ISBN: 978-1-950730-08-7

Poems

I.

Girlhood	9
Snow White Without the Seven Dwarves	11
Rapunzel I: With Rapunzel	14
Helen I	16
Goddess of Whores	18

II.

Helen II	21
Rapunzel II: Why I Locked Her Away	24
Rapunzel III: Aubade as Rapunzel	26
My Life in College Told as a Fairytale	28
Eris's Thoughts While Crashing the Party	31
Mrs. Zeus	33
Persephone, let me tell you about Death	35
Tricked to Wrath	37
Becoming Seafoam	49
The Priestess Responds	52
Foam Proposal	54
A Deal Complete	55
As Captive	56
Beauty Contemplates the Birdseed	58
A Promise to a Monster	59
Forgiving the Stepmother	62

III.

Don't Say Don't Be A Girl	67
Carving Out Prince Charming	68
That Which Bound Odysseus	70
If All Horses Were *Sleipnir*	73
Burning Feathered Wings, Burning Wax Wings	74
Self-Portrait as Spring Maidens	76
Helen III	78
Glass	80
A Loud Message	83
Tomorrow is Winter	85
Sacrifice	87
The Feminine Fairytale	89

I. Her lips were frosted with sugar and faeriedust.
—Allyse Near

Girlhood

In response to "The Pomegranate" by Eavan Boland

During my teenage years I lost
My belief in Fairy Tales and pixie dust,
But came to see myself as Persephone:
You know, the prolific goddess bearing
Corn from dawn till the sun retired
Behind the meadow's horizon, waving
Back a promise to my mother to return
With fresh flowers of golden and rose
Hue in each of my tender hands.
                        But what if
I didn't return?
An odyssey cut short by the seductive
Sip of pomegranate wine. A date
Above the land where the dead
Wander gray fields,
Or a winter behind bars.
Would she, Demeter,
Give an ultimatum to bring me back?
Neglect crops until I return?
Roam the countryside
And leave it barren in her careless wake?
In this manner she and I are as one,
Caught in the trial that is girlhood

Where we can't escape.

In this season between girlhood
And womanhood, where the chance of me
Fleeing is ever increasing, she is as constant
As the monument built to honor her—
Gazing skyward, arms extended, revealing
To the heavens a countenance weathered
With lines and shadow.
There she'll wait like the stem waits
For the Narcissus to blossom,

Tilting her ear towards the hardened ground,
Listening for laughter and footsteps racing unrestrained.

Snow White Without the Seven Dwarves

I. The Huntsman

      Imagine the night and thorn-kissed princess
So delicate that her
Delicacy transforms into
Meekness.
      Imagine her skin, contoured
By violet smudges, exhausted beside
The cold stacked stones of the wishing well.
      Imagine the huntsman, a spy.
The Queen wanted thoroughness,
      So even his axe has eyes.
He whistles an empty melody
But hears a full song
When she screams.

II. The Cottage

      Imagine Snow White without the Seven Dwarves.
The cottage is empty. Raw potatoes with spotted skin.
Washing and folding a forgotten tradition.
      The little men weren't aging
When they knew the cottage,
When they didn't know Snow.
After their mining days,
After picking and swinging,
They gave it up—
They hauled their lives
Across the next mountain
Range and chose the sweetness
Of retirement.
Snow drags a bucket
Of water from the well
Three times a day,
And the bruises turn yellow.

III. The Prince

Resting in death,
Again an innocent. Only in death.
        Her throne a wooden
Coffin.
        By chance, he meets her.
The top of her head was wet
From syncopated
        Rain.
How he's wished to know
        Her lips,
They're waxy with death.
If he holds his breath,
Hovers his hand a hair above
Her lips,
He feels a tremor
From her skin.
        Give it two years and she'll flick her eyes
        Towards every passing soldier.
        What will she want next,
Following her resurrection?
Seven men all to herself?

Bless the poison.

All the same, she lives.

Rapunzel I: With Rapunzel

I am hidden   Back between
         The mountain next to the stillest river
And the one so high it has conversations
         With the clouds.   Sometimes the pines
Anger the stomach of the hanging wisps
         And it rains on the tower roof.   In this cylinder
I have my favorite pie recipe,   Cherry and spun cream,
         My favorite brush,   It loses seven bristles
Every moon cycle,   And my softest apron,
         With my name embroidered in red.   The stitches are
Spaced a fingernail apart,   Missing the first two letters
         Punzel, Punzel.
Mother rocks in a chair at the edge of the forest,
         A speck beside the winking pond.
Sometimes I see a salmon jump sideways,
         But there's no splash.
She brings me berries and rosemary,
         That's when I ask about the salmon.
The water from the well was all
         I drank,
And she told me the salmon drink it too.
         My, my, a landscape so green and blue
I'd smear the colors under my nose,
         But I can't reach their taste
From my perch,   So once I climbed the vines.

   They caught my hair And ripped a strand.
Once I tied a message to a stranger's wings,
   But the thing cried and twitched
So I held it like I would a dripping handful of blueberries,
   Then to the soil-pot of some saggy gardenias
I steered its beak and watched it peck.
   I pretended we both had teeth and mimicked its nibbles
With nothing to chew but air and saliva.
   Eventually I bit a petal,
And it melted like sugar.
   The sweet was the smallest maze of relief
In the space I was built to live, Guarded by married brick
   And cement, Where swallows dive between the open shutters.
When mother returns, I tuck away My shiny whispered dreams.
   I say the light outside is much too bright. Stay with me By the fire.

Helen I

This morning I met a friend,
A little goat bathing in a sunspot
Outside Persephone's vacant
Temple. Its eyes dim hollows
Like faded coins or the shadows
Between the folds of marble statues.
Perhaps it was a misstep—
That led its hoof to a divot
In the dirt.
I saw it stuck,
I saw it tugging—
Oh, useless! Useless girl I am!
If only my hands were not chained
By girlhood!
But then—as if Persephone had
Compassion similar to her sister
With the bow—it tore free from the vines
Of nature's prison. It nudged a rock,
Uncrossed its legs, and bounded
Beyond my sight.
The terrain was so solid I wanted
To ask how its hooves followed
The path of its flock; if it had always
Straggled but yearned to lead
A stampede down a mountainside.

Instead, I called out to my brother
Some strides down the slope,
And my voice echoed like a war cry:
Brother, let us return home!
How I crave...
But I could not finish.
Home stretches as far
As I can find creatures
Who do not speak the language of man,
Who bleat so clear,
Who cry with me,
With my mouth ever so human.

Goddess of Whores

Yes, dear maiden. Rest your eye upon the goats and horses.
They need your tending. Do nothing else lest it be permissible.

If you meet an *Aphrodite* in a dream,
Along the shore of Cyprus
Swelling from a silver scalloped seashell,
She will already be bursting.
Ask her to share a mouthful
        Of oysters or figs,
Then beg to feast upon her heart.
        She'll give you the ripest artichoke.
You'll still bite into it. Savor only heaven.
        Then you wake.

For the maiden, duty and purity are wedded. Her story stays as such.

II. *If I am not an ocean, I am nothing.*
—Shara McCallum

Helen II

When they speak of me,
It's with a measure of confusion;
Unsure if my heart was wicked or my
Head dumb. Want the secret?
Why I so hastily fell
To the Trojan Prince's bed?
It was the jewels
He bore, the gold
He wrapped around my wrist.

Oh no, I fell in love
With the drought I brought,
The one that made me water.
My power became a vibration
Felt by my husband.
Every man that touched his hand
Knew how I'd beg during sex—
And they wanted his head
In payment for the dry-spell.
Only miniscule entertainment,
But entertainment nonetheless.

You will not get any easy answers here.
Bring me more gold,
I will not reveal why I left.

But perhaps it is a mystery
Better suited to you, so sip
Some wine and imagine the ship trimmed
With lanterns radiating over the water.
Do you imagine I slept
In a bed or in the prisoner's cabin
Surrounded by moldy wooden beams?
Take the hint. Draw a conclusion.
Try Aphrodite for some answers,
Even the Golden Apple
Might pose as an oracle.
All causes will lead to one final answer,

That beauty makes value invisible.
My talents of speaking—
Oh, the deals I would strike!
Even my gold is pulled away
By sway of the Golden Apple.
Do not, sister, express
With your voice
What should be heard
Solely from your body.
That is called *obedience*
And we dance to it on tiptoes.
The title of *goddess* belongs
To the home and to the bed,
But not to the coveted
Treaty table shoulder-to-shoulder

With kings. They're the ones
Who will retell my myth
And claim *this is what every*
Woman is like.
Only then will my face be clear.

Rapunzel II: Why I Locked Her Away

I locked her away because
She was me and I've never
Regretted the deed, but I won't
Chant along with the petty mantra
That witch! Hideous hag
With chipped and misshapen teeth.
We start with the herbs and how
I coveted them. I wasn't the only one
Who did. When a child was my reward
For relinquishing five sprigs of spice,
The payment satisfied my tongue
Like baked apples sprinkled
With cinnamon. So she's locked away.
My name is *Mother* and my stories
Are what I keep from her—
How I danced to a bard's fiddle
In the market square and he kissed
Me twice after the final note.
I locked her away but left fresh tarts
Beside her flower pot and watched her savor
The crunch of the buttery crust.

With my womanly touch
The sugar is helpless,
For we can eat it without

Teeth rotting.
Farwell cleansing, farewell dirt.
What I didn't have was
A predator's eye.
I never saw his hands—
They were green! A quiet tree.
Daphne didn't dwell within me—
I couldn't grow leaves or morph
My skin into bark but the herbs
That covered my back, the *rapunzel,*
Tickled my nose and kept
My heart in silence.
The plant smells strongest
Beside the river, beside the jumping
Salmon. I care for its growth
The way I care for her.
I'm already an hour late for dinner—
Been lost in a meadow looking
For some sweeter berries suited for pie.
She'll burst through the walls
Beaming, bright, famished.
Together, we'll bake and salivate
As two wild bears.
She'll eat it all and forget
The great world's poison.
Together, watch us smile.

Rapunzel III: Aubade as Rapunzel

I'll escape to my tower on horseback,
Maybe a dappled horse, a noble one
From which I'll see flowing springs
For the last time, their banks lined with
Violet bellflowers, herbs, and willows.
I'll lock myself away this very morning
And behold forever the gleam of
Sunrise from a tall, narrow window
Framed with sturdy beech-wood.

Here, will I busy myself with painting
Roses and glowing stars in the sky.
Here my only companion will
Be my hair: weighed-down curls
That reach beyond the mile-high
Drop of the tower.

Here, no man with false intent will
Scale the aged bricks to win my heart.
No gallant Prince cradling a violin
In one arm and gripping a broadsword
In the other will captivate me with
A graceful bow or an innocent extension
Of his hand, and even if one should wish to dare
The climb, I'll leave the surrounding gate

Fastened tight with indescribable iron
Shrouded in fog that won't give way to light.

I'll lock myself away so I may awaken each morning
From a dream of you wandering through
Thickets of brambles with thorns
Catching and tearing your fingers that
Once roamed over my neck and shoulders
Searching for the tower,
Seeking release in the nearby river.

My Life in College Told as a Fairytale

Once upon a time, I was a damsel who stumbled into the path of chariot-driving villains.
And *once on upon a time* I could've thrown away my crown like a bride tossing her flower
Bouquet. I never saw the consequences of prideful radiance.

I swear I prayed better than a nun, though I never felt the tap of a Fairy Godmother's wand
On my shoulder. Watch, I will still wait. Prayer is only wasted belief.

Where the old lady failed, I invented a genie.

First wish:
To become a daring daughter of fantasy. Let me become deaf
Before the *evil stepsisters*. Give me this one immunity so I don't become trapped by their
Laughter.

I am not on a quest. Despite turning in every direction none have come to me and I'm without a
Compass.

Second wish:
To know why most princes come disguised as kings spitting gold when a better definition is a *barrel-bellied tavern glutton.*

A good pour of witches' brew over their rusted silver tongues and they
    still couldn't scratch the surface of attractiveness.

I wish I didn't have to compare them to monsters because there's no
    instruction manual for
A monster's defeat and because it's becoming standard to call a prince a
    beast. How about—
If not boastful princes, then something that shames nobility. Fresh
    hypocrites.

Third wish:
Just bring me a dragon to fight the next one in line.

I am writing this because I cannot say who I am without a thousand
    scrolls. I cannot locate
My tower or my hairbrush.

I realize I wasted my third wish. I only need my scrolls to have wings and
    vocal chords. I only
Need them louder—those parts of me that are the most beautiful—my
    nose and fingers, my
Calves—let them reach further.

A pen can sleep. So will I if I prick my finger on a spindle.

And I am not far from a *happily ever after.* What did *Sleeping Beauty* say?

"I've seen him so many times."

Yes, I have seen it—this Fairytale end. It is not far. I can plant its seed. I'll make it unbroken.

It was the thing I caught a glimpse of when I fell in love with the traveler from the woods—for with him I think I know a flying carpet.

Eris's Thoughts While Crashing the Party

The irony in being a servant
Of guile is to taste iron,
But not command from
Which fell body it flows.
I've watched many a hollow
Party sing from the clouds.
My duality of obedience
And patience is over,
Which is why I choose to play
With libation and women.
They're practically treading
Through a vineyard—
I could raise vines
To pin their ankles to the floor.

Then the moment came
When I approached a different fruit for help.
I've been asked what the golden apple
Actually was. Was it gold molded to mimic
An apple? Or was it an apple with mutated skin?
Either way, the taste stung like fire.

Aphrodite is a lost ship
In a masculine sea.
Like her sister, Athena is so close

To madness she could be a queen.
Hera is a face. She likes the quiet and feathers
And none of us are gentle.
I am one of them.
I suppose because we are pirates,
We are not quite women
As we should be.
A sword will always be sharper
Than a party invitation. Remember that.
Hold on—I have furniture to converse with.
Bleed and covet, soaring goddesses.
Bleed for me.

Mrs. Zeus

Rarely queens   are virgins to vengeance.

    They spy within clouds   and bristle at women

With emeralds snaking   around their necks.

    She's a trickster hiding   with games and riddles,

And she'll outsmart the deceit.   Think of the one known for peacocks

    And screaming at Zeus.   Once she terrified Thunder

When he twisted a mistress's locks.   It was then she saw sun

    Blaze from his fingertips   and melt mist.

Behold what happened   in the absence

    Of a wife's forgiveness!   She transformed the dreamy

Girl and made the sun white,   made limbs into hooves,

    And from the facial structure   protruded a snout

With massive flaring nostrils,   as the emerald beads squeezed

  And squeezed the pendulous neck. A first grave made for the cow,

Arid and icy like the moon.

  I think it's fair to ask if Hera was offered a tomb,

Or rather a pyre for her virtue so sacrificed.

  Mistress Hood is a cycle with one leading lady

Playing the role of scorned, and the one below her

  Is also below the husband. After fiddling with retribution,

She's called to the next man and dresses him

  In turquoise feathers with gold circling blue centers.

Persephone, let me tell you about Death

Oh, if I could halt time
At the rise of spring,
My fingers would resist
The winter wind.
      My Persephone, my love—
With hair like the
Pomegranate,
You are what I covet.
A passing year doesn't stretch you,
Where age is my mind's doom.
Let me hope beyond myself,
Let me live in halves—
Fresh and scentless
Then sour and frosty
Under leaves and snow—
If you promise I never grow
A season older.
Still, if the colorless rose
Is comfortable in death,
      I wonder why am I not?
Aging is a canoe with a hair-strand
Sized leak
      As I hasten to Hades.

Now, in the midst of a cheerless
Winter Solstice; I listen for you—
Remember dreaming of a child?
That was me who cried,
Wishing my body to become as yours
And my mother's as Demeter's.
We live a reality of absence
You haven't discovered you know—
Being plucked out of the sky
And out of myth with a rake.
   Persephone, listen
To the plea of mortality
And be shocked by death.
   I learn you only give in halves
Because your legend is black and white,
   And therefore wrong.
I feel your breath descend upon my ice-stung ear
To soothe envy's bite.
   You say
We'll both be found in a tomb—
You with the worms,
Me in a nightly tapestry.

Tricked to Wrath

"Hapless Orion fell by the cruel virgin's shaft and now fills Chaos."—
Valerius Flaccus

I. Artemis Dominion

When you touch the night,
You touch Artemis.
The taste of her poison,
The shimmer of the moon in her crescent-shaped eyes,
      And
If by chance you encounter a stag of hers,
Run, shoot, or meet your end by horned fury.

II. Orion Dominion

With eyes first opened on the hills of Boeotia,
The infant hunter rose as a Titan with ready bow in hand
To rival the Sun God
Shining in his hair.
  He could be a giant,
   Clenching an arrow from point
To feather and crushing it in his grasp.

III. First Meeting

"Artemis took him [Orion] away from the sight of mankind" —
Antoninus Liberalis

Imagine a chase,
The nymph's tunic train
Racing ahead of him.
      This Daphne he pursued assumed
Herself to a willow tree.
While not lured,
He and the Moon Goddess met eyes and raised bows.

IV. Two Archers

Mortals never dared race them on their hunts.
        The archers grappled for kill,
Aiming and launching,
        A poor stag's   last humble breath and twitch
Before an arrow.

V. Brother, Do Not Look At Me So!

The first to be foolish was Actaeon,
        A moment of gaping   then devoured.
The second was you.
        Ah, it is those selectively
Barren that are the most   enticing.
        Your eyes belong firmly fixed
On laurels,   hear their call.

VI. Orion Dreams of The Scorpion

What dream is this? That I should return to sleep so often graced
By visions of the moon goddess,
Her legs over my hips as I dissolve her title of Maiden,
    But tonight
Impenetrable armor envelopes her scaly form
Until her stinger grazes the farthest corner of
My heart moments before dream's end.

VII. The Birth of a Trickster

Candaeon was a rape myth,
        Yet what
If all men in his image stood a lie in dust?
        Though cold and merciless, nothing could move
Her revenge more than harm to virgin or child.
            Sitting beside a riverbank, Apollo sings the lie of how Candaeon
            Yanked the legs of a favored high priestess
            Apart
To a favorite melody on his lyre, so
The lyrics traveled to his sister's ear.

VIII. After the Dream

Heartbeats before Orion's awakening
From the most stomach-churning dream, to birth
      It roared.
They wrestled first with fist then shoulder,
His heels carved hollows into soil as he was pushed closer to the
Sea's edge until warm salt foam tugged at his shoed feet.
On the opposite shore stood Artemis.
      Tricked to wrath,
Her arrow flew.

IX. Constellation

Through all this, where were her animals? The rabbits and owls and cubs.
Surely they heard the mellow notes plucked from her brother's lyre,
      Surely,
      Surely they knew.
      Perhaps they exist as they always have,
Dumb beasts who stood and watched powerless as
Zeus raised the giant corpse from Poseidon's arms to hang as
Stars only revealed at her time.

Little Mermaid

Becoming Seafoam

Find me singing in a seaweed
Grove to a school of mackerel,
Where every surface—solid
Or liquid—is slimy.

When asked why I gave
Up shouting through a hurricane's
Winds to call a sailor home,
I defended my shy throat,
Answering *perhaps tomorrow*.

I could not lure and awe
Humans to captivity and death—
I suppose a measure of charm
Was lacking—
So I become one of them
And met my end.
      With my sisters, the sands
      Of beauty sifted to me
With pouty shrimp lips.
The coated clams lifted their shells
As if I was some sort of heroine,
And *Ensnarer of Mackerel* became
My honorific. Why did the forage-fish
Power and nestle between

the strands of my hair, drawn
To my voice? Because I
Couldn't kill with pebbles

And sea-stars chiming.

To trade fins for feet
And pay the debt
With a voice-box,
The reward needed
To outweigh the gamble.
Fit me with toes to hold
Snail caves
So the burn is not so strong,
But don't give me shoes,
  No, I'll never dance
  Like a bashful maid,
  I want to be a savoir
  But that role was stolen—

It was you, my dear Virgin Temple Girl,
Whose greatest sin was sacrificing
The blood of bleating animals. You
Wore the blue cloak
Of heroism and leapt
Into strong arms, swept away
Like crab legs at low tide.
Not some poor beggar;

A vivacious wife and bringer of vitality.

The gift from my sisters
Was a dagger dipped
        In love.
Because I didn't use the blade
        The way they pleaded,
I left him on the goatskin cover
And you in your white nightgown.
Because I let your throats
Stay sealed and not spitting
Forth jelly and fish guts,
I am now the fizz and hum of waves serving
As your lullaby,
The seafoam that rubs against the dirt and sweat
Eager to soothe your swollen ankles during
Your final months of pregnancy.

The Priestess Responds

Princess, I don't think your worst sin
Could outweigh mine. Do you know
Why I maneuvered him over the altar like a sail?
At sunset, housed among hanging herbs,
A familiar intruder split the temple
Curtains and didn't finish with me
Till I heard the stars' heartbeats
Fade to slumber in full darkness.
Two pinches of flaky thyme,
Plus a palm of dried parsley
Disguised his meat as a burning
Ram's. I had nothing left to do except release the sheep
Into the hills beyond. I'd dare not disturb their blood.
Now the two-faced moon leaves my dreams
In peace.
      My faith is best placed in you.
Seafoam does not mean statue.
For once, I shall make a demand. Rewrite your claim, sister,
That I have but one sin. The role of savior was one I never
Sought. My wettest kisses are yours. Bless your hand
For forfeiting the dagger. You ask for distance,
And I will be a palace gate blocking your hatred.
      I carry a daughter.
        She is the sun. She sends the ocean winds from
The north. She cries for miserable souls lost beneath

Plough's brightest star. She cries for you. She feels
Your essence. Your touch is how my breath hitches
When I dream of flight.
When she first crawls, it'll be towards
Bountiful arms reaching from a horizon
Where rape is in its final oblivion.

Foam Proposal

If it heals you, imagine
I've lingered over your sorrows,
For I have—even but for a moment.
I've witnessed a lone lightning
Strike swamp a sturdy ship,
But four fail to fracture another.
You have an ally
With arms in the ocean.
We'll carry this pestilence
Like horses slapping
Away flies with their tails.
Our wish will take force
By a deluge,
For there is no illusion
Made reality more feared
Than sisters disguised
As a terrible thundering hoard.

A Deal Complete

Raise the knife once more
And make it steady—
Divide the pack and
Calm my daughter.
Send their lungs
Stuffed with seaweed
And sand to my shore
In an empty whiskey bottle,
And the blanket I wear
Will never again bear thorns.

As Captive

I saw the cracks of winter
Thaw in my mirror moments
After you gave me the library.
How quickly I became myself
Again when there was that
Familiar reflection—
And I couldn't betray my world
Any further by continuing
To deny it wings.
I stopped letting the maids
Dress me in petticoats—
Ladies, would you care
To find another princess?
I'm only his freshest
Captive. I am reluctant
To call them *family*
While my father
Sits at home
Mourning the rose
He dared to bring me.
They are more like idols,
With breath a furnace
That heats my neck.
May the leather spines
And oak pages

Shake into horses
On a warpath
That lead me
To words,
So I may ride
Through a river
Of ink,
The hooves
Telling me
How tonight
I will kiss a wolf.

Beauty Contemplates the Birdseed

A curious wingman was the birdseed
You clutched in your claws—
Who knew it would be minced corn,
Gold like pixie dust
That drew me to your paw
After the second snow.
The first melted in haste,
But the next was soft enough
To make slippers out of.
    Tell me, have I taught
    You well of delicate creatures?
Five red songbirds met, hovered, curious
For a dozen or so wing-beats before plummeting
And your frown lifted when their beaks
Began to peck at the nourishment.
They, who cocked a head
And muttered were not
The only critters with wings
You released at the first sign
Of breakage. Now that I have
Been spared from snapping, I believe
The snow is made of diamonds.

A Promise to a Monster

Should I be goaded by sisters,
Begging that I remember our happy jests
While tapping powder
On our cheeks before a mirror—
I'll still return in a week's time before
The window panes become locked
In ice forever. They're odd girls,
I'll admit. They'll invent tears
By rubbing onions in their eyes.
That water is fiction.
I do not want them
To sulk and dream
Of transforming my eyes
To a target for dart practice—
I want them to admit their envy
For ivory garments I wore—
The ones he covered me in—
The ones that crumbled
To rags like a pricked
Finger on a rose thorn when they
Grabbed at the rebellious fibers.
"How dare you bring
Such a wasted color!
Give me precious pink."
But see, pink is rare

In faded hearts. It remains
Loyal only to roses.

They want to keep my fingers from melting
The snow off of wilting flowers.
I know this, because once I would, too.
I am intrigued by this thing
Called jealousy—
Was it the hooves
They found threatening?
No, it was the hooves
They found enticing,
Flowers eager to be trampled on.
Because they could not take my place,
Because they're the essence of infatuation,
Because they cannot save
A wheezing monster,
They'll kill him.
      Women,
Do not be in such a hurry
To claw your sisters' hearts—

And for a prince—
Spread your arms
Upon a wooden stake.

      Still my promise is concrete.
To save you from breaking,

I'll slip through the night to return
To you my body.
To you, still a wolf—
To the gate where my skin
Will glow when your fangs are near.

Forgiving the Stepmother

Mother, I have a solution
Then you can find a pale path
That doesn't know your name.
Tomorrow I will water your morning
Glories. I will keep your garden's last turnips
For soup. You ask for a map. For shoes.
The walls of this house
Remember as elephants do.
I say they saw too much
And will not let you stay,
Like the looming trees
Of a fairy realm—
Their leaves are ears, branches eyes—
They pick sides during war,
Remembering every cry over
A twisted wing.
Go to them, that horned wilderness.
You will be surprised how eager
It is for you.
Follow the eight-toed cat
On a chase while I meet a new
Dance partner named *Forgiveness*.
Should you meet a walking cloak
On the road frosted with autumn,
Answer that you are a wanderer.

From hill, to meadow, to fairy-grove,
Ask for shelter and it shall be yours.

III. A woman who loves a woman is forever young.
—Anne Sexton

Don't Say Don't Be A Girl

Don't say don't be a girl,
Because when you say *girl*
You mean a fossilized flower.

Don't say don't be a girl,
If by a girl you mean a doe-eyed deer.

Don't say don't be a *Sleeping Beauty,*
If by a *Sleeping Beauty* you mean forever prone.

Don't say don't be a *Goldilocks,*
If by a *Goldilocks* you mean pinched-up and unsatisfied
With her position in the Milky Way.

Don't say don't be a girl,
Because you want a girl to be ragged
And lacking a crown.

Don't say don't be a girl,
Because the girl I am
Didn't cross the evolutionary
Bridge to favoring a sword of steel
Over a sword of flesh.

Carving Out Prince Charming

I don't love that man
Any more than I love
The hunk of marble
Before my knife,
Because that couldn't
Possibly give it spirit.

Carve Prince Charming
From this that already
Exists.

Forgive me, but I cannot.

All I know is he wore
Both shoes from sunrise
To sunset.

      One-dimensionality is no crime—
To exist beyond the realm
Of tender attachment,
To be slapped
With a handsome face and nothing more—
      So what!
I'd gladly open my arms to any man,

Prince or stable-hand—
    Better a simpleton than a rapist.

That Which Bound Odysseus

I. The Oath

Should've been broken.
        Oh, the serpent
You could have been.

II. The Man

If you wanted glory,
You should've cracked
Granite. Or you could
Challenge a god.
They anger like bulls.

You should have been a sculptor
Or a wood-crafter.
When you make a horse
For your son on his eighth birthday,
He'll order it to battle
And its legs won't crack
As real horses' do.

When you return to home and peace,
You're recognized only by the colorblind
Eyes of your dog with nobody to bring
Bread, meat, and a blanket
And say—*your hands are cold,*
My lord. Would you care to command mine?

III. Conclusion

It is inclination to dissatisfaction
That compels relocation.
Seeking the quickest stag
Or a war so loud.
I can say that humans
Want to be where they
Are not.

I am not compelled by greed
For godhood, yet the lavender
Scent of sensual loyalty
Might spur me to action.
In our restlessness, we could
Meet on the same battlefield.

If All Horses Were *Sleipnir*

No matter the cushioning soft ground   or bed of fresh fodder,
A horse will die   after losing a leg.
It can rest but when the flutter   of robin's wings coming
From a nearby bush reveals   a charge of spears,
A sling   and some plaster are useless.
When they're prompted against instinct,
Eight legs might mean luck,   because the oppressive
Weight would tip like a seesaw   over the four legs.
Four minus one   and it's a failed trilogy.
But if all horses had eight legs,   when they're touched
With swords the limbs would still beat,   the solid iron veins
Increasing thousand fold   Instead of sinking into muck.

Burning Feathered Wings, Burning Wax Wings

Behold a Father, midwife to his creation,
        Forging wings for a lesson
That isn't worth learning because it's death,
        Make him accept condemnation.

His hair is singed under the thatched roof,
        Here is where he keeps his props,
Still in the womb.
        He stored an extra pair of wings
With his hammers and fire props.

The son wailed because
        The pigs, the horses, both bulbous
And greedy, bored him with their monotonous
        Grazing and staring.
So he asked to be a bird,
        Wings with colors
Swiped from the rainbow.

They flew and bathed in clouds.
        The thunder quieted and the lighting
Paused to keep their skin from igniting.
        As the son flew too high the wings

Bent, cracked, and then blazed
    In a circus-like plummet.
When wax burns it hangs like vomit,
    First reluctant liquid then stiff
Until it's melted and molded again.

    When wings burn
They're ash, ash, ash.

    The father keeps awake all night and chews
    His cheeks to forget the hunger
Hammering at his stomach,
    Pounding like Athena at Zeus's skull
Before bursting forth.

Self-Portrait as Spring Maidens

I cannot pause in pleasure over
Having found a sunning daylily—
Because I can already see
The cycle of winter coming
In the veins winding around my wrists.
Like Persephone, I escape and reappear.
The dirt is best when it's wet,
With the buds beneath the surface ready
To shimmer around an abandoned wire fence.
Like Perdita, I have found a source for a better garden.
The cross-bred flowers were at war.
They fought metamorphosis.
I'd plant seeds and watch them sprout and open—
They did, but choked each other
Before rotting. The wild ones shut quicker,
But when they came back were fuller
And covered the meadow like haze
Covering the sky. I used my skirt
To gather little yellow petals before
They turned brown. In those moments,
I forgot what it meant to be silent.
Ever wonder why we die in winter?
I do. The answer is forever as simple as
We're prettiest as newly shaken
Tulips from the earth.

In spring, we smell like marigold water.
Two birds always swirl
Above my head in opposite directions—
One headed for our myth born from Eden,
The other to the dirt to share pomegranate
Seeds with the worms.

Helen III

I learned in the halls of Ilium,
There are things we make
We cannot fix.

I learned that from my husband
After he skinned leopards,
He'd pull on the teeth
And squish the paws
While gazing, almost wondering,
Beast, can you hear me?
Can you see my grin?
Hear the lilt in my voice
As I boast that your coat
Is with me and not covering
Active muscles?

The hide led to conversation,
And in his drunkenness
He wailed that he chose
The wrong goddess
Because a wife should
Not be made of war.

I stayed bold in my silence,
Musing on our parenthood,

Mother and father to every
Solider cramped between
Creaky ship quarters
Twitching their thighs,
Singing that home
May just be a foreign whisper,
Groaning that they are thirsty.

I learned from me how I might
Just be the earliest story
Of *woman* and how a *woman's*
Face is fatal or forgotten.

It is too late to reflect
On power and accountability,
But finally the chains fled.
In time the city faded
To a gray scar,
And the drought
Escaped to the ocean.

Glass

What I love about fairytales
Is that objects can be heroes
Or villains. Even if morality
Means nothing to sculpted glass,
It can still build a fate—
May I call it *the price of love?*

> *Virtue*
> /ˈvərCHoō/
> Noun. Behavior showing high moral standards.
>
> *Chastity: The wedding ring replaces the belt.*

Without virtue, the glass slipper
Operates as a shiny lady

> *Temperance: She doesn't know why the stepmother yells again, but she won't yell back.*

In a ruby headdress
Slipping around a masquerade,
Waiting to be a snake.

Call it the Atlas
Of her resurrection—

Charity: You'll never know her sacrifice.

It raised her up from abraded
Knees, soot-filled palms ,
And a stomach the size of an acorn
To a silver balcony
From where she hears gunshots
Echoing from hunters shooting
Peasants, but the feathers
Won't stick under her nails.

    A MAID NO LONGER!

Vice
   /vīs/
   Noun. Immoral or wicked behavior.

Or we can say the glass
Was a hasty trickster

   Kindness: She'll never maneuver against him.

And picked her rose too fast.
*Princess, there is work
On your knees calling!*

> *Diligence: The floor is still smeared with mud? She'll scrub it again.*

Happily Ever After! You were saved
By glass—we say congratulations.
Hold Onto Goodness, her mother would say,
Cradle it tenderly like a newborn
Lamb. Don't break this, take good care—
Protect! You'll need it.

> *Humility: Say your rose is the reddest and it crumbles.*

It won't run off and break.

> *Patience: She waits for the right beast of burden to share the load.*

A Loud Message

Dear *Lovers* and *Friends* alike—
We believe *happily ever after*
Is something to clutch fast—
For longer than a year, or two,
Whenever the honeymoon
Becomes foreign sand.
I say it doesn't mean a promise,
It means the biggest wish
Like we forgot our shoulders
Can't carry its load unless
We have a water buffalo handy—

I think whoever can out-burden the buffalo
Should teach others to be warmer and louder
About love and the inevitable decline
Of the honeymoon's white shores.
If that were me, I'd promise that *happily ever after*
Isn't sudden—charge to the roses and away
Retreats the redness.

But maybe the *ever* is the barrier
Here—*happy* is a welcome guest
And *after* comes like the seasons'
Endless and predictable cycle.
It's *ever* that's uncertain,

And almost a challenge—
Because we want to walk in stride
With lazy butterflies instead of digging
Our oars into the river to keep
From pitching down the waterfall.

When I say *happily after*—
Happy after the rain, down the waterfall,
Happy with and without the oars—
I mean that we were joined by both bright
And dim. What sickened and healed us.
Let's remember that sometimes our shadows
Can accumulate to a rainbow,
Even when we're tossed by a tempest
And can only survive by cowering
Between two barrels of gunpowder.

Tomorrow is Winter

> *It is winter and the stars are hidden.*
> *- Eavan Boland, "The Pomegranate"*

When I stopped dallying in girlhood
And realized our legend was wrong,
I could not keep my hands from reaching
Or my back from hunching and pressing
Against the temple walls that leaned towards
Your absence, mother—
I needed to keep them sturdy.

I have known paradise
Before a thousand sunsets.
Every time the wheat tops
Turned to follow our approaching footsteps
We were reminded that our flame
Was immortal, but recently I have
Been shocked at death so real
And eager to be joined.

I face what I cannot remember
But that which I know is true—
That when I was born, you slept
In a bed of sickles and prickly stalks.
When I rose with the first indigo tulips,

I was your little flower crying
For nurture and the sun.

I finally understand the alternative
To permanence—do you hear
The world and the silence
That's everywhere but where
We are? From this point on,
I will do nothing but *cherish*.
For one more sunset,
We will stay in the meadow
In company with drying stems
Swaying against the sky
Just barely tickling the fading stars,
Teasing us that you will soon
Be draped among them.

Sacrifice

There is a story from mountains
And glowing northern lights
About how the cosmos began
A new light from the center of an
Ash tree because Odin peeled his
Eye from its socket and dropped
It into the cocoon of a well.

There is a story of knowledge—
Of what should be as hidden
And married to the dark runes
As tree roots.

There is a god with a neck elegant
Like the arch of a stallion's—
Bearing a stolen brand
Of numbing comprehension.

What if I could cut
Out limitations by cutting
Out my eye?

See, most are happy without
A Viking's heart but still pleased
To know there are souls who

Have one. I don't fast
Before war though I go to it.
I don't want my name
Carved in rooted caves
Or behind stars conversing
With secrets.

But as I write this, I feel waterfalls
Rush through my legs
Because I am in mourning
For women who broke rocks
And were broken on rocks,
Who carried fire in their palms
But moaned until death
By its blaze.

Their sacrifice was gladiatorial—
A Prometheus quietly doomed.
They cut burdensome heart
Of domestic task only to grow another
Duty, prepared again for use.
Do I dare ask you—
Can you open a history book
And point to where women were
Not just immortal platters
Ready to perform
Evolutionary necessity?

The Feminine Fairytale

Heroine

/ˈherōən/

Noun

>   1. *The chief female character in a book, play, or movie, who is typically identified with good qualities, and with whom the reader is expected to sympathize.*
>   2. *A woman admired or idealized for her courage, outstanding achievements, or noble qualities.*

"*I used to be Snow White, but I drifted.*" —Mae West

Snow White Woman:
Has been written
Like winter because winter
Is cold and delicate
But will melt
Under a warm touch.　　　　　　*Not Snow White Woman:*
Famous for a controversial　　　Is on a newer page
Non-consensual kiss.　　　　　　And tumbles in the too-dirty
Perhaps she should have risen　Sheets and escapes the virgin essence,
On her own.　　　　　　　　　　　But still a woman. Bright. Eager. Strong.

Princess

/ˈprinsəs, ˈprinˌses/

Noun

    1. The daughter of a monarch

Informal

    2. A spoiled or arrogant young woman

Let's begin placing her
Behind Fairytale bars
Where everything is white.
Look for the lock pic
Between the bed sheets.

She [Princess] lives:
In a cottage under circling crows,
Inside a tower with hay for drapes,
By the banks of a silver-tainted stream
Clear for lusty followers to find,
Or inside flowers peeling open at the sound
Of Fairy laughter,
Then in seeps rain to dampen wings.

She [Princess] wears:
Mist, dandelion seeds attached
Like snow to a horse's mane.
If not in nature's robe
Then in drapery of plum,
Cardinal, and midnight blue.
Never britches, never a blouse.
Pink
Always better than gray or beige.
Oh, the dread to be mistaken for a man!

Weak

/wēk/

Adjective

> 1. Lacking the power to perform physically demanding tasks; lacking physical strength and energy.
> 2. Liable to break or give way under pressure; easily damaged.

She is too weak, too arrogant

Too noble, too pretty

Too unable to resist the

Prince

/prins/

Noun

> 1. The son of a monarch.
> 2. A man or thing regarded as outstanding or excellent in a particular sphere or group.

He's learning to be outstanding,

To touch, so he seizes

The hem of her skirt like a philosopher

Clinging to a dream of Plato.

As yarn unravels under needle and bobbin,

From a previous incarnation

She has evolved—that fair

So frail existence

Characterized by wolves

And magic spells.

Please, don't return her to the cell.

When did she drift?

                        When she was rewritten.

Evolution

/ˌevəˈlooSH(ə)n/

noun

> 1. The process by which different kinds of living organisms are thought to have developed and diversified from earlier forms during the history of the earth.
>
> 2. The gradual development of something, especially from a simple to a more complex form.

The Princess was a jewel within pages,
Now she combats the ink
That kept her locked in a tower.

Dear Princess,
Dear Woman,
Where do you stand now?
Would you prefer to be rescued
From a spell? Somehow being a dove
Became a shame—I want to know why.
The seeds I plant in your brain will form lilies.
You will be an engine. Or a flower. Or both.
Or neither. Surprise me.

In the new *once upon a time*
In the new *happily ever after*,
She renounces a gold ring
And weds steel.

She is too strong, too changed
Too tired of being tethered

To fear what they say
About witches.

Should she change, should she not? Ask her.

> *Was Snow White afraid?*
> No doubt.

> *Is it beautiful to drift?*
> Quite so.

> *Is a princess braver to fight a stepmother with words or an army of gladiators with a bow and arrow?*
> They are equal.

> *When a tale is rewritten, is it better than before?*
> Depends on what it says.

> *When a character is rewritten, does she stand above her former self?*
> Again, ask her.

She says:
Let me veil my head in flowers,
Strap songbirds to my shoulders,
Breathe in lemongrass and roses,
And stay how I'm written.

> *She says:*
> Let me drop the crown over
> An ocean-side cliff and pick

Up a blacksmith's hammer
And chisel for a business of Muscle and clang.

She says and keeps on saying.

About the Author

Pomegranate Odyssey is Hannah Calkin's first book of poetry. She graduated from the University of Maine at Farmington with a Bachelor of Fine Arts in Creative Writing in 2018. Her work has been featured in the *Sandy River Review*, *The River*, *Barren Magazine*, *Persephone's Daughters*, *Rhythm & Bones*, and *Riggwelter Press*. She currently lives and works as a tutor in southern Maine.

About the Press

Unsolicited Press is a small press in Portland, Oregon. The progressive publishing house was founded in 2012 by editors who desired a stronger connection with writers. The team publishes award-winning fiction, poetry, and creative nonfiction.

Learn more at www.unsolicitedpress.com.

www.ingramcontent.com/pod-product-compliance
Lightning Source LLC
Chambersburg PA
CBHW020126130526
44591CB00032B/541